THE COP
and
THE SPIRIT

Harry Kartinen

ISBN
978-1-958122-94-5 (Paperback)
978-1-958122-95-2 (eBook)
978-1-958122-93-8 (Hardcover)

TABLE OF CONTENTS

ROGER IS LOST

One afternoon while working as police officers in uniform my partner and I received a radio call about a lost child. We drove to the address given us and contacted the parents of the lost child. They stated they were from out of the area and had come to visit some friends. Their son Roger had gone to a local school to play with the children of the people they were visiting.

When the children came back Roger was not with them and everyone went to the school where they had been and looked for Roger. After a complete search they could not find Roger and it was starting to get dark. They then called the police.

I was the senior officer so I called in several other units and the helicopter and a police dog. I assigned everyone an area to search and then my partner and I went to our area and began to search. I was driving and I began to think about my son who was the same age as Roger and all of a sudden a compassion I had never experienced came over me. I thought if it was my son that was lost I would want the Army, Navy, Marines, Boy Scouts and just everyone looking for him. I then recalled that the word of God says he has given us his Holy Spirit and all things are possible to those who believe.

At that moment I asked Jesus, if it is true and is for us today as I believe the word says, then help me now, where is Roger? Instantly I knew where Roger was. In my mind I knew that I knew that I knew where he was. The Holy Spirit told me Roger was standing on the northeast corner of 68th St and Orcutt Avenue, and there was a group of children standing in a circle and Roger was standing in the middle of the circle, and he was crying.

I was driving, and without saying a word to my partner I headed to 68th St and Orcutt Avenue. As we left our search area my partner reminded me that I had assigned the search areas, and I was violating my orders to the others not to leave their assigned areas. I told him I knew where Roger was and we were going to get him. As we turned north on Orcutt from Artesia I pointed out to my partner the children three blocks up at 68th Street and Orcutt Avenue. As we pulled up there on the northeast corner was a group of children standing in a circle and in the middle of the circle was Roger crying.

We picked up Roger and took him to his parents. My partner asked me if I was part bloodhound or what? The Holy Spirit told me to keep silent and so I did. I then thought this is good and I want more, lots more, and I asked how to get it. The Holy Spirit said to seek first the kingdom of God and these things will be added unto you. Do not seek the gifts or the benefits but seek my face.

This was the first time I was used by the Holy Spirit and was just the beginning of years of adventures in the spirit.

HE IS IN THE TREE

I was working afternoon patrol when an armed robbery occurred at Pacific Avenue and Willow Street. The suspect had entered a restaurant and pulled a handgun to rob them of their money. The suspect ran west on Willow and then north. We had thrown up a perimeter and were sure we had him surrounded.

One of my old partners who was a K9 officer came to the area. Just then a lady called the police and stated her dog was barking at something in her backyard. Her dog was in the house and it was dark outside. Her address was within our perimeter so the k9 unit and I went to the lady's house. I went because I knew the dog and the dog knew me. We told the lady to stay inside and keep her dog inside.

We went to the side gate and after giving anyone in the yard a chance to speak up or give up we entered. The dog was turned loose and he ran towards a huge tree in the middle of the yard. Suddenly, the Holy Spirit told me to point my shotgun up into the middle of the tree. As I did a voice in the tree was yelling "I give up don't shoot."

The suspect stated he had a 44 magnum and it was loaded; it was in his front waistband. I told him to come down very slowly and we took him into custody. He was on parole for armed robbery and said he was going to shoot the dog and k9 officer. When I pointed the shot gun right at him he gave up. He stated "I'm not afraid of any handgun but only a fool would argue with a shotgun."

HOPE RESTORED

I was working uniform patrol when I received a call about a possible attempted suicide. I went to the address and contacted a middle-aged woman in her apartment. She was lying on the sofa and would not get up. She seemed depressed and had an "I don't care attitude." Her daughter had called the police after talking with her on the phone. The daughter was at work and I called her to find out why she was concerned about suicide.

The daughter stated her mother is a diabetic and last night they had taken her to the emergency room of a local hospital. Her illness was out of control and her blood count was way above normal and dangerously high. Her mother was released from the hospital and had an appointment with her doctor at 1 pm this day. The daughter stated she and her brother were coming to take her to the doctor later but her mother sounded so depressed and seemed not to care about living that they called the police. Part of the problem is that her mother does not eat and her blood sugar level gets all out of balance. She tried to talk her mother into getting up and eating but her mother refused and said she did not really care to live.

I talked with the lady and between the fact her children had grown up and were on their own and she had no husband and her diabetic condition, she just lost hope and will to live. She stated she would never kill herself but she did not really care about living.

I called the hospital and her doctor and confirmed her appointment and called her daughter and son back and did all I possibly could within the scope of a police officer. I told her I had to leave and my duties as a police officer were ended but as just a person who cares could I have her permission to pray for her. She said yes and I knelt down by her as she lay on the sofa and prayed a very direct and pointed prayer for her healing and spiritual renewal. I finished the prayer and got up to leave when the lady jumped up off the sofa and said "I feel good." She got up and said she was hungry and she was going to cook herself some food. I left.

A few months later I was patrolling down her street when I saw the same lady standing on the sidewalk.

She looked at me and began yelling "Police, Police." It sounded like a person calling for help. She had a big smile on her face and came up to my car and asked if I remembered her. I told her I remembered her. She said "You changed my life that day and I wanted to thank you and have been looking for you ever since." I thanked her and reminded her it was Jesus not me and she said she knew that but I brought the message to her. I talked with her a few minutes and left.

HE IS WAITING

One morning as I was getting ready to go out on patrol in my black and white, I was at the rear of the car putting my briefcase in the trunk when the Holy Spirit spoke to me. He said to go to 17th Street and Lewis Avenue because there was a man wanted for murder standing on the corner. He told me the man's name and said he would wait for me. I looked to my left and saw one of my old partners at the trunk of the car. I told him that at 17th Street and Lewis Avenue there was a murder suspect standing there and I was going to go get him; I asked my old partner to come along. Without hesitation he said yes.

I went to the area and walked in and spotted the murder suspect and radioed to Bob and we moved in. The suspect was arrested without any problem.

It is approximately three miles to 17th Street and Lewis Avenue from the police station parking lot where the Holy Spirit spoke to me. As always the Holy Spirit was right on target.

THE CHICKEN BANDITS

I was assigned to the robbery detail and my partner and I were working night detectives. We were at Hill Street and Atlantic Avenue about nine one evening. I had just spoken with a crime victim. I had been driving and as we turned on the engine the radio came on. The dispatcher was putting out the facts about an armed robbery that had just occurred at 4th Street and Ximeno Avenue.

There was a group known as the chicken bandits that were robbing only chicken takeout type eating establishments in the area. My partner was one of the assigned detectives to the cases and when he heard the radio broadcast he said it was them again. At that instant the Holy Spirit told me to go to 7th Street and Junipero Avenue because they were going to rob the Pioneer Chicken at that corner. I was told not to hurry and the suspects would wait for us to arrive. I drove at normal speeds and did not hurry. We were in a four door tan police detective car with black wall tires and a radio antenna sticking up like a flag pole. Anyone could tell it was a police car.

The Pioneer Chicken was on the northeast corner of the intersection and directly west across the street was an auto repair garage which had a blacktop parking lot. You could not see anything on the lot and it seemed to be the perfect place to park but the Holy Spirit told me to go to the southwest corner which was a Safeway Market lot. The lot was empty and the parking lot lights were on but the Holy Spirit told me to park in the lot by a light pole. As I stopped the car my partner, a surprised look on his face, asked me if this was where we were going to stop. When we left Atlantic and Hill I had told him that they were going to rob the Pioneer Chicken and we were going to catch them.

This seemed to be a stupid place to park but I followed the direction The Holy Spirit had given me. I turned off the engine and reached to get my binoculars from the back seat. I put them to my eyes and there they were, walking in the front door and wearing the same clothing they had just worn in the robbery approximately 40 minutes earlier. They used the same method: one has a sawed off shotgun and he takes all the employees into the walk-in freezer and takes all the money from the front and back while the other stands lookout in the front.

We radioed for backup and then I drove our car across the street to the dark auto repair lot. We waited for the suspects to come out and they walked right up to us because they could not see us. We took them into custody and all the employees came outside. They stood on the sidewalk applauding. If we had pulled into the same lot they would have seen us and could have driven away; we might not have seen them. The Holy Spirit had to have blinded them to our car because anyone should have seen us in the lighted Safeway lot and should have seen us drive across the street into the auto repair lot.

By following the exact instructions of the Holy Spirit, even if they seemed a bit unusual, I have found out that everything works out perfectly.

THE MOPED RAPIST

I was working uniform patrol on the day watch and had stopped to have a cold A&W Root Beer when one of my old partners called me on the radio. Dennis was now a detective and was working sex crimes unit. He and his partner met with me. Dennis told me he did not know why he was going to tell about this case except he felt he just had to.

A woman had gotten off the bus after work and was walking home when a man took her at knife point and forced her down an alley into and underground parking area where he raped her. The woman did not know the suspect but she had seen him in the area before. He'd been riding a moped. The description of the suspect was very general and there were no identifying marks or anything unusual. He was an average guy and his description fit a lot of men in the area.

After Dennis drove away the Holy Spirit told me to go to 14th Street and Cedar Avenue. As I pulled up to that intersection I saw 8 or so men standing on the grass. About 30 feet from them were 4 or 5 mopeds. The Holy Spirit showed me one man and one moped, indicating the man and the moped of Dennis' case. I stopped my car and radioed Dennis to come. I stepped out of my black and white and pointed to one man. He looked at me as I pointed to a moped. I asked him if that was his moped. He said it was and walked over to me. I asked him if he had a driver's license and he gave me a California license. He stated he'd just gotten out of jail and all his warrants had been cleared up. I wrote down his information and he walked away as Dennis drove up. This man lived here one night, there the next, and was unemployed. I told Dennis that was his man. He took the information a left for the station to get a picture of the man from the records division.

The police report indicated that the victim should be at work now, but Dennis said something told him to call her home. When he called she answered and said she had not felt well so she had not gone to work. Dennis took a photographic lineup to her and she made a positive identification of the suspect as the man I had pointed out to Dennis.

Dennis got on the radio and told me what had happened and asked me where we would find the suspect. I told him we would find the suspect at 10th Street and Pacific Avenue. I was on Pacific Coast Highway and Chestnut Avenue and Dennis was somewhere south of 10 and Pacific. He came north on Pacific Avenue and I went south of Cedar Avenue towards 10th Street. I got to the 10th and Cedar intersection and looked east. There was the suspect pushing his moped. He had run out of gas. We stopped and arrested him.

I do not hear a voice I just know that I know what I know and there is no mistaking the Holy Spirit when you get to know him.

SHE LIVES

I was working uniform patrol in a black and white patrol car on Anaheim Street at Cedar Avenue about 3 PM when I got a radio call to go to 12th Street and Deforest Avenue. The call was a 927, unknown trouble, a code 2, no red lights or siren but hurry. I acknowledged the call. Then the Holy Spirit told me to go code 3, red lights and siren; so, I did.

When I arrived there were several people standing by the county flood control and they said a little girl had drowned. I called for medical aid and lifeguards. I went up the bank of the flood control and looked in. In the middle of the flood control there were two men doing CPR on a little girl. I made my way out to the men. As I approached the men stood up and they had the most terrified looks on their faces. They did not know CPR but they were doing the best they could.

I got down on my hands and knees and examined the little girl. She was laying on her back. Her eyes were open and the pupils were fixed and dilated with no response to light change. Her skin color was ash gray and she had no heartbeat. She was not breathing. The two men said she needed CPR. At that instant the Holy Spirit welled up from within me and told me to pray for the girl, speaking life into her. The Holy Spirit gave me the words. As I was on my hands and knees directly over the girl looking into her eyes then I spoke the words: "In Jesus name I command your heart to start beating and I command your lungs to start breathing. I command all of your vital organs to start working, and from the top of your head to the bottom of your feet I command every fiber of your being to be restored to perfect health. Little girl live."

She began breathing and her heart began beating. Her color started returning. I could hear the fire department arriving; they came out and took the little girl to St. Marys Hospital.

I interviewed the two men. They had been working on a loading dock when two little boys came up and told them that the sister of one of the boys had gone into the water to get their dog which had fallen into the flood control. The dog got out but the girl had drowned. They went into the office and repeated the story; someone in the office called 911 and the two men ran to the little girl's aid. They saw her in the water not moving. One of the men went in and got her out. They did the best they knew how to give her CPR even though neither of them had any training.

Later I went to St. Marys Hospital emergency room and was told which room she was in. I rounded the comer to her room and saw a doctor walking out with his head down. He was telling the nurse that he couldn't understand what happened. He knew she'd drowned but there was nothing wrong with her, no effect at all. There was nothing wrong with her but they kept her overnight.

I then heard a little girl's voice coming out of the room: "Ouch; that hurt. I want my mommy."

IN CUSTODY

One morning at the squad meeting before going out on patrol I was reading a sheet with the violent crimes that had occurred the day and night before. I came to one rape case that had occurred approximately 1 am; a man had crawled through a window and raped a woman. The Holy Spirit told me the name of the suspect and after the meeting I went up to the detective division and found out that one of my old partners was assigned the case. I gave him the suspect's name and left.

Because it was night the victim did not get a good look at the suspect but the suspect had left a partial print on the window sill. Plus, a neighbor had seen the suspect enter the window. The neighbor did not think so much about it, because in this neighborhood it is not uncommon.

The neighbor did not hear any screaming. So she did not think anything was wrong.

The detectives went to the scene and talked with the victim. They found out the lab tech had a partial print. They gave him the name to see if they had a match. When they found out there had been a witness they got a picture of the man I named and put together a photo lineup. After showing the photos to the witness she made a positive identification; she had seen the suspect in the area before. The lab tech also advised the detectives that he had made a positive match on the prints.

The suspect happened to be on parole for the same crime and was living only three blocks away. By 3 pm that day the suspect was in custody.

LARRY'S BURGLAR

One day I was asked to help arrest a known, wanted burglar on a warrant. Larry found out where he was and five of us were going to go get him. My job was to come down the alley and cover the back door. I told Larry to give me plenty of time to get into position and I would let them know on the radio when I was in place. It would take me some time to get to my spot and they were to wait. I went to my spot and as I got there I heard that they did not wait and had already hit the house.

When I got to the back door it was open and the suspect had apparently fled when the others came up the front. Larry apologized for not waiting and we all left.

As I was walking down the alley the Holy Spirit told me the man we came to get was on the other side of the gate where I was, and if I called him by name to give up he would come out. So, I called his name and told him to come out. The gate opened and the man walked out to give up. I put him in handcuffs and we walked out from between the buildings into the alley. Down the alley were the other officers. They came looking for me when they did not see me in the alley.

Larry walked up and pointed up into the sky and said, "It's not fair you had help didn't you?" I told him exactly what happened and I took my handcuffs off the man. Larry thanked me and took the man to his car. As I drove out of the alley Larry stopped me and said "I don't know what you have but I want it. I'll be in church Sunday."

I KNOW WHERE
YOUR CAR IS

I was on day patrol in a black and white when I received a call to meet a man whose car had been stolen. Upon meeting the man I found out he was from out of state and was from Utah. He was driving a company car and it had been stolen.

The reason for his weekend trip was to visit a well-known homosexual club in our city. He told me he was married and his wife was at home with their children. She did not know he was homosexual. He had met some young men and they had taken his wallet and car. He did not want to file a report; he only wanted the car back. He said he would be fired if his employer found out he had taken the company car out of state. I advised him we should file a robbery and auto theft report, but he refused. He only wanted the car back.

The Holy Spirit immediately told me where the car was parked. I told the man to get into my car. When we started to drive off he asked where we were going. I told him I was taking him to his car. He asked how I knew where his war was. I told him I'd explain it later.

We drove about four blocks and there was his car parked at the curb. There was a hide-a-key and gas credit card so he knew he could now get home. He had no money for food but he did not care; he just wanted to go home. I filed a missing wallet report to cover his credit cards and driver's license.

Again he asked me about how I knew where his car was. I explained that the Holy Spirit told me where it was parked. The Holy Spirit told me to tell him that this was his last chance. He thanked me and a fear came over him, not the kind of fear of getting hurt but a deeply rooted fear in his soul. I felt a change in him and he even had a different look in his eyes. I cannot explain it; I just saw it and felt it in my spirit. He got into his car and left for home.

I have no concrete proof of this, but I strongly feel that he straightened out his life. It's just a feeling I have. I know that when the Holy Spirit moves through me that good always comes out of it.

THE FUGITIVE

I was on patrol in uniform and a black and white when I saw a man go into a low-grade hotel where drug users and trouble makers hang out. I would normally go into this hotel two ro three times a week and it was time for a stop there. As I entered the lobby there was the man I saw go in and the Holy Spirit told me to just get to know him. I struck up a conversation with him and over a period of weeks learned his name and a few things about him through these casual conversations.

To my knowledge he had done nothing wrong. I never inconvenienced him by stopping him or detaining him.

One day about 2:30 pm I got a radio call to return to the station to see the captain. When I got to his office he introduced me to two FBI agents who were looking for a man wanted in Chicago and was thought to be in our city. They showed me a picture; it was the man the Holy Spirit told me to watch and get to know. The captain asked me if I had any idea where to look for the man; the Holy Spirit told me to go to the back door of the hotel and the man would walk out.

I said "Yes, I know right where to look." Let's go get him; the agents said, "Now?"

We took my patrol car to the hotel. I drove to the back door as instructed by the Holy Spirit and as I stopped by the back door it opened. The man walked out and right over to my car. The FBI agents showed the man a picture of himself and took him into custody. The whole thing took about thirty seconds.

The FBI agents were pretty amazed about the whole thing. They never said a word, but when I said "Let's go get him", they were amazed.

It is not my job to judge or punish but to catch the evil-doers. Thanks to the Holy Spirit many of them got caught.

THE STOLEN
MOTORCYCLE

I was assigned to uniform patrol division, day watch. I was stopped at a stop sign on Linden Avenue at Anaheim Street facing south when I observed a motorcycle going west on Anaheim with two people on it. The Holy Spirit told me the motorcycle was stolen.

The motorcycle started to turn left going south on Linden Avenue when the driver and passenger looked at me, obviously nervous. They started to make a u-turn to east on Anaheim and as they turned I noted there was no license plate on the motorcycle. As they turned the motorcycle stalled; they fell over in the middle of the street. I helped them up and move the motorcycle to the curb.

It took only about two minutes to determine the motorcycle was indeed stolen. The two crooks went to jail. Don't tell me God does not have a sense of humor.

CODE 3

One night on patrol in a brand new Ford police car we got a call to go code 3, red lights and siren. I was driving east on 10th Street; we had a fresh green light ahead of us so you would not be concerned about cross traffic. As we approached the intersection I did not see anyone and all the traffic had pulled over; everything looked good. The Holy Spirit told me to stop, so I did. My partner looked at me like "what are you doing?" Just then a car going south ran the red light going about 80 miles per hour.

Instantly we knew that if we had not stopped we would have been hit on the driver's side of our car. My partner, who looked a little pale, asked "How did you know?"

THE DOPE HOUSE ROBBERY

While working afternoon patrol I found myself driving around this one block. The Holy Spirit said to just keep driving around the block. I drove to the corner and turned left, then to the next corner to turn left; just kept doing this. After going around the block twice my partner asked me what I was doing. I told him we were to keep going around this block and that something was going to happen.

After our third or fourth time around the block gunshots came from a small apartment building. Two men came running out to the sidewalk. One of them had a blue steel revolver in his hand and the other had a brown paper bag. They ran right towards us and then split up with one going one way and one the other. We knew this was a dope house and figured it was a dope house robbery. We chased down one of the suspects, but the other got away. We recovered the brown paper bag which contained money and dope.

We returned to the scene of the crime and contacted the man who lived there. We knew the man and his family, having arrested his son before. He stated he and his sons were at home and two guys came to buy some dope; they were selling them some dope when another knock was heard at the door. They opened the door and two other guys said they wanted to buy. So, they let them in. After they closed the door one of the men just let in pulled out a revolver and demanded everyone to lie on the floor. Everyone got on the floor face down. The two men robbed the man and his sons and the other buyers.

After they got the money and dope they started to leave when one of them said "Let's shoot that one." The man with the gun shot the man lying by the front door in the head and left, firing another shot. The man who had been shot was face down. After the suspects fled the man who'd been shot and his friend jumped up and ran out the door.

We checked with a local hospital and found they had the man who'd been shot in the back of his head. Before going to the hospital we looked where the man had been laying and saw a tear in the carpet. Following the tear, we found the 3 8 caliber slug. We kept the slug and went to the hospital.

At the hospital we spoke with the gunshot victim. He admitted he was in the apartment to buy dope when the other guys came in and robbed them. The bullet had struck him on an angle and had torn his scalp then continued down toward his back, entered the skin above his left shoulder blade, pierced his body and exited just below his shoulder blade. The doctor bandaged him and he was out of there.

We booked the one suspect for attempted murder and armed robbery, and began looking for the other one. We knew what he looked like, but did not know who he was. In about two weeks we found out who the other suspect was and where his girlfriend lived. We knew his movements but couldn't grab him.

One night at the end of our shift, 2:30 am, the Holy Spirit told me to wait until 3 am and then go and get the suspect at his girlfriend's apartment. We had a warrant for his arrest so he was fair game. We waited until 3 am with assistance of six other officers we surrounded the apartment and I went to the door. I knocked and a female voice asked who it was. I announced it was the police; we could hear running in the apartment.

Other officers reported seeing window shades moving. After about two minutes the girl came to the door and I told her why we were there. She gave us permission to come in. I found the suspect between mattresses in one bedroom and arrested him.

As we were taking him out of the apartment he stated it was not a legal arrest because I got off work at 2:30 am and it was now 3 am.

HERE IS YOUR STICK

When I began working afternoon patrol at the Long Beach-Compton border I knew it was going to be a challenge. It was common for rocks and bottles to be thrown at the police cars at night. It was a rough area. The first night I was up there we had stopped for a red light at 69th Street and Long Beach Boulevard. I had my window down as usual and said "Good Evening" to four or five young men at the corner. That is all I said. As the light turned green and we drove off a couple of bottles came at us from the rear. I told my partner to just keep driving. We began arresting the local gang members in Long Beach and Compton; I always looked them in the eyes when I spoke to them and always called them by their proper names. They were treated with respect and dealt with fairly. How would I want to be treated is how I treated them. My partner did the same.

After about six months I knew just about all the local gang members and had been to their homes to meet their parents. Whenever I arrested one of them I would always go to the parents' home and explain what had happened. The gang members ranged in age from 14 to 28 or so. After about a year I was treated by them in a very friendly way; I loved all these guys. I did what I could to encourage them into better lives. It got so that if any of them was wanted for crime they would not run or fight with me anymore. In many cases I would just tell their parents and they would surrender.

One night we heard shots and drove up on a robbery and assault with a deadly weapon in progress. We caught two of the suspects right there; the third got away. We knew the third one, so we went to his mom's house and left a note with her to call the police tomorrow when her son comes home. The two we caught said they did not know it was us; they just saw a police car and ran.

The next evening we were getting our car ready for patrol when a day shift officer came and said he had arrested the other suspect. He said he could not believe it when he got the radio call to go and pick up a man wanted for armed robbery and assault with a deadly weapon. He went to the address and the suspect's mother told him that I had been there last night to ask her to turn in her son. She gave him a note with the crime report and all the information he would need to do the paperwork. She said I told her to give this to the officer who came to get him. She then called her 25 year old son out of his room. He surrendered. This officer could not believe what was going on and that he would just give up because I had said he had to.

Now, about the stick. I had been working up in that area for about a year when one night about midnight I spotted a guy we wanted. I told my partner to stop the car and I got out. The man began to run and I told my partner to drive around the alley and cut him off. I chased after him on foot. He ran through an apartment complex and I was right behind him. As I grabbed a chain link fence to make a quick right turn my night stick got stuck in the fence. I let the stick go and continued after the man. He ran between two buildings, trapped. He had to go through me to get away. Now, we are in an all-black area and the man I am after is black; it's midnight. The only two white people around were myself and my partner.

The man came at me for a fight. I knocked him down twice when about twelve of the local gang members showed up. They had seen me run after the man and followed to see what was going on. As the man was getting up to come at me again the leader of the gang held out my night stick to me and said, "Here, do you need this?" I told him no and asked him to hold it for me. He asked if I needed any help; I said "No." He then said that he had sent one of the boys to find my partner and bring him here.

This time the man came at me and I knocked him down again; he did not get up. We took him into custody and took him to jail.

I learned that I did not like what these guys did, but I loved them. Jesus taught me to separate acts they committed from the person. It is written "I will cause your enemies to be at peace with you."

OUR POLICE

We were on patrol in a black and white; it was about 6 pm. I was driving and we had just cruised down an alley. We turned towards Long Beach Boulevard when we observed the manager of one of the apartment buildings fighting with a man thirty years younger than he. We knew the manager and he is a good person, never does anything but good so we figured the other guy must be a troublemaker.

We stopped; they stopped fighting. The manager said that this man and his friend were in his apartment courtyard trying to sell drugs. The man did not have any drugs on him and was not wanted so we told him to go back to Los Angeles and stay out of this private property. Well, he had an attitude and lost emotional control and started a fight with me and my partner. He thought he was a real tough guy. It took about two seconds to get him under control.

My partner was handcuffing him when the man's friend came out of the apartment complex. When he saw his friend being arrested he got mad. He noticed that there were about twenty gang members about ten feet away watching. He tried to incite the gang members to help him take his friend from us and beat us up. As he was yelling the leader of the local Cript gang, who was in the crowd, stepped in front of him and all the gang members moved between us and him.

The leader said to the screaming man "These are our police and if you want them you have to go through all of us first." This even surprised me because this happened on a public sidewalk on a warm summer night with lots of people out watching. I knew these guys liked and respected me and that I loved and respected them. But, for them to openly and publicly stand up for two white police officers is a big thing.

Needless to say, the other guy was dumbfounded and left. I am sure he was stunned. We took the other to jail and from that day on those gang members did look out for me. When we parked our patrol car they guarded it. When we were on foot patrol in the neighborhood they walked with us.

Jesus sees us and loves us and he also sees the dumb things we do. He does not like it, but he gave us a will and he just keeps loving us and forgiving us when we ask him to. He also knows that there are consequences for our actions and he will help us with that. When I learned to separate a person's actions from who they are, it changed my life and let the love of God begin to really grow in me.

HE TURNS HIMSELF IN

I was assigned to the robbery detail and had just arrived on Monday morning for work when two homicide detectives told me that a gang member with a certain street name had killed another gang member on Saturday night. They asked me if I knew what the real name of the killer was. All they had was the street name. I gave them the real name and his home address.

One man killed the other because he had hit up his girlfriend for a date and it made the killer mad. He waited in ambush and shot the other man to death.

The homicide detectives wanted my help in arresting the suspect. I called the suspect's mother and she said that her son had gone to his father's house which was about fifty miles away. I explained to her that we were going to arrest her son for murder; she understood. I offered to pick her up and take her with us to get her son; she refused and said that she would call her son and have him come home to turn himself in. I told her we would like to go get him now, but she would not tell us the address. She said she would have him get on a bus and come home, and that tomorrow she would call me at 10 am to tell me where to pick him up.

When I told the homicide detectives they laughed at me and made fun of me all over the detective floor of the building. They did not believe that a hardcore gang member who'd been in jail many times and was wanted for murder would turn himself in. I really did not blame them for having doubts, but they sure made fun of me all day.

The next morning at 8 am the homicide detectives were in the robbery office laughing at me some more. At 10 am the two detectives returned to the office and pointed out that it was 10 am; where was the phone call. They really got on my case and went back to their office laughing very loudly. No one thought that the phone call would come, but I did because the Holy Spirit had told me yesterday to call the suspect's mother and that I had done the right thing.

At 11:15 am my phone rang; it was the suspect's mother and she said the suspect was at home. She had not called at 10 am because she cooked all of her son's favorite foods and had a party for him. She knew he would probably never come home again. She said her son was waiting for me and they both wanted me to come get him.

I went into the homicide office and was greeted with laughter and unkind comments. One of the detectives was leaning way back in his chair with his feet on his desk. I let them make fools of themselves for a while and then said "I thought you might want to go get him with me, he is at home waiting for me." The detective with his feet on his desk fell over backwards and had to catch himself. You should have seen the looks on their faces. They asked if I was kidding and I said no I was going now. I walked out of their office. They came out after me and said I could ride in their car with them. Suddenly, they were nice to me.

We drove up to the suspect's apartment building and parked in front. It was not a good neighborhood but it was my old beat and everyone knew me, so we were safe. When we got out of the car the detectives asked me if the car would be okay. There was one of the gang members there and he said hello to me. I asked him to watch the car. He said no one would touch it.

We entered the apartment courtyard and went up the steps to the suspect's apartment. The homicide detectives had a picture of the suspect. They checked it with the people in the courtyard. We walked along the second floor walkway and went past the suspect who was kissing his girlfriend. The door was open; the suspects' mother invited us in. The party was still in progress. I introduced the detectives. They asked where the suspect was; I told them they had just walked by him outside. They instantly turned towards the door when the suspect walked around the corner and entered the apartment. He said hello to me and that he was ready to go. The detectives had a hard time believing what was going on.

We said good-by to the suspect's mother and left with the suspect. At the police station the homicide detectives took the suspect and interviewed him. To their surprise, he told them everything.

From then on things were a little different between me and the homicide detectives.

THE GOING
AWAY PARTY

It was 2:30 am, time for our shift to end. We were working uniform patrol in a black and white. Instead of calling us out to go home the dispatcher told all units to remain in service due to the large number of service calls being received. It had been a warm summer night and very busy. We had been on the streets for 10 hours and were ready to go home.

About 3:30 am we got a call to go to break up a loud party. Four other units were sent with us but we were the ones in charge. We were told that officers had been there twice before in the evening and asked the people to quiet down. As we drove up I could hear music from about five hundred feet away. There were people standing at the curb with car radios going and drinking beer in public.

The source of the party was coming from an upstairs apartment. We went to the apartment; the door was open. The apartment was jammed with people. I knocked on the open door and some people near the door asked what I wanted. I asked to speak with the person who rented the apartment. They said to wait, then slammed the door.

They were drinking and appeared to be just about drunk. Their attitude was hostile. I noted that the other units had arrived and the officers were talking with some of the partiers on the sidewalk, trying to get them to leave and turn off the car radios. All the party goers were black and all of the officers were white. By the body language and the stances, the officers were taking it was obvious that trouble was brewing. There were ten of us and about two hundred partiers.

Finally a black woman about fifty years old came to the door and said it was her apartment. We reminded her it was 3:30 am and the party was too loud and must end. I asked her what the party was about and she stated her daughter just graduated from a four year nursing program and was leaving today for her first job in Texas.

The Holy Spirit told me to congratulate the new nurse and get some common ground with them. In my heart I knew what I was going to say was what I really felt as I know nurses and it is something to be proud of to finish four years of school; God had given her a desire to help others. We talked for a couple of minutes and they became friendly.

At this point I could feel the anger between the party goers and us. I prayed for peace to overcome everyone in Jesus' name. Instantly there was a clam that swept over the entire area. I noticed the other officers relaxing and the partiers doing the same.

I then pointed out that it was after 3 am and the neighbors had their rights to peace and quiet. I pointed out that it did not appear as though any of the people really seemed to care about the reason for the party but just wanted to party. I stated it would be a sad ending if we had to break up the party as this was a night she would remember forever. The woman who rented the apartment was the graduate's mother and she agreed with me and so did her daughter. They said they would end the party. Within fifteen minutes all the people were gone. Everyone left quietly, being very friendly towards us.

It is just one of those things that you had to be there to see for yourself. One minute you could cut the hostility in the air with a knife and in an instant a peace swept over everyone and I mean everyone.

THE FAMILY FIGHT

I was working day uniform patrol when I got a call about a family fight. The caller stated her husband was drunk and had several guns in the house. I contacted the woman and her child about a block away. She said her husband beats her up and scares their child; all she wanted to do is get into the house for some clothes for her and the child. They were going to stay with a relative for a few days. She planned to divorce him and also get a restraining order. She insisted she was going into the house to get the clothes; she wanted me to come inside with her. I asked her what kind of guns were in the house, where they were kept and if they were loaded. She told me where all the guns were and that they are loaded.

Along with other officers we went to the house. I went to the front door; it was opened but the screen door was locked. I listened and heard the husband come into the front room. He was drinking a bottle of beer. When he saw me he yelled at me and wanted to know why I was on his property. I knew there were two loaded hand guns in the front room and I could see the drawers they were in. He walked towards the front door which moved him further away from the guns.

I calmly talked with him. He was drunk and not in control of his emotions. He was dangerous. I explained that his wife wanted some clothes. He would not allow his wife or child into the house.

His wife, who was not the kindest person in the world, began yelling at him and talking about a divorce. I quieted her down and tried to calm him down. It was no use; you cannot reason with a drunk. He got louder and louder. He finally said "What's the use?" He began walking towards an end table where one of his hand guns was kept. His wife saw where he was going and said something about him going for a gun. She grabbed her child and took off.

The screen door was locked and I could not break it down in time to stop the husband. But, I could not back away and leave a drunk, dangerous man with a gun. I knew I could kill him easily; did not want to do that. I just said "Jesus, no help me."

By this time the husband was at the table and was bending down. His right hand was reaching for the drawer with the gun. He froze and did not move for a couple of seconds, then straightened up and backed away from the drawer, never touching it. He turned around and said "You seem like a reasonable man. Let's talk about this." He walked over and unlocked the screen, inviting me in.

He no longer staggered; his speech was now clear. He was not drunk anymore. I talked with him and his wife came in. They made up. We settled the matter and I left. I worked that area for years and never again got another call from those people.

ALLEY ROBBERY

I was going to work one afternoon about 3:30 pm. I was riding my little Honda motorcycle. About two blocks from the police station the Holy Spirit told me to turn down the alley west of Pacific Avenue and go south from 5th Street. As I proceeded down the alley the Holy Spirit told me to turn right in the intersecting alley. As I turned right I saw a young man run up behind an old lady and he reached around her to grab the purse out of her hand. He pushed the lady downward and tried to pull the purse from her. Before he could push her down I had him in one hand the old lady in the other. I helped the lady stay up and arrested the suspect. The lady was not injured and the guy went to jail.

37 STAB WOUNDS

I was working a one man plain clothes unit on day patrol. At 20th St and Long Beach Blvd the Holy Spirit pointed out a man and said to watch him. I followed and watch for a long time and finally caught him sell drugs. I arrested him.

I took him to the station and was at the booking desk with the suspect when a homicide detective walked by. He stopped and took me aside. He asked what I was booking the suspect for; I told him.

Turns out they were looking for him for the murder of a security guard and needed to question him. Worked out perfectly. The security guard had been stabbed thirty-seven times.

HE NEVER HAD
A CHANCE

I was working uniform patrol on the day watch; it was a beautiful Saturday morning. I immediately got a call to take a dead body report and was told that the fire department had already left the scene. I was told the victim was 99 years old and the fire department stated it was natural causes.

I drove to the address and pulled up; the Holy Spirit told me the old lady had been murdered and the girl sitting on the front lawn knows all about it. I contacted the girl who told me she lived with the old lady and took care of her. When she got up this morning she went to check her and noted she was not breathing, so she called 911.

Leaving the girl outside I went inside to stand at the bedroom door so I could see the victim. I noted she had a four-legged walker and all of her things appeared to be where she could easily reach them. On the floor was a jewelry box and one of the drawers was open. I could see where it had been on a dresser and was now out of place. I looked at the victim and noted some strange markings on the left side of her neck. I did not touch her. I noted some dark specks on the wall behind her. Her bed had an open headboard.

I requested the homicide detail and went out to the girl. She was still crying. I asked her if anyone else had been in the house last night. She said only her and the old lady were there. She asked why I asked; I told her the old lady had been murdered and we would have no problem finding the killer. She then cried harder and got a scared look on her face.

The girl's sister lived a couple of doors down the street and she came to see if the girl could come to her house. I got their names and told her it was okay but not to leave as the detectives were on the way. They would want to talk with her. The house was now sealed as a crime scene.

As I waited out front for the detectives and lab man the girl's sister came back and stated the name of the person who did it. I asked "Did what" and she said "Killed the old lady." She said the man is her sister's boyfriend and he stayed there last night. He killed the old lady and is now sleeping on her couch with blood on his shoes. She again repeated the man had killed her and he was on her couch. She wanted me to come get him immediately.

I could not leave the crime scene unprotected, so I called for assistance. Two units got there in about one minute. I sent them to arrest the suspect.

The Holy Spirit also told me the victim had been raped and when the coroner got there I told him, but he did not believe me. As he conducted his investigation I again told him she had been raped and as the investigation progressed he told me I was right. He asked me how I knew because he could not believe anyone would rape a ninety-nine year old lady.

This suspect never had a chance because the GOD sees all. The detectives stated that it was a good thing I got the call because anyone else would have gone along with the natural causes. The crime may have never been discovered.

THE TERRYLIN
PLACE BURGLAR

It was about 10 pm when my partner and I were on patrol in a black and white. I was driving when we heard some other units get a call for a burglar inside of a house. There were two units dispatched and another had called in that they were also on the way. The call was several miles away and we were in our beat, listening to what was happening. I heard one unit radio the station that they were on the scene.

Then the Holy Spirit told me to go to the call with the other units. We took off to the address on Terrylin Place. As we listened on the radio it was apparent that they were having a hard time locating the house. The third unit called the others and told them how to get to them. The talking back and forth between the units alerted me to the fact that they were on Terrylin Circle, not Terrylin Place. I tried to tell them but they were busy talking to one another, so we just drove to the call. I advised the dispatcher that we were on scene at Terrylin Place and told the other units that they were on the wrong street.

We contacted the person who called and it was the son of the people who live there. He stated he came home from work and opened the front door, seeing his stereo equipment stacked by the door. He went to the kitchen and saw the window broken. He listened and heard someone crawling on the floor upstairs. His parents live on the second floor and he lives downstairs. He said his parents don't crawl on the floor. He said his parents are home and should be in bed. We noticed other items stacked up in the kitchen. It was also apparent someone was still in the house.

We went upstairs. It was pitch black at the top of the stairs. We stopped and listened, hearing someone crawling. We got to the top of the stairs where there was a large double door into the master bedroom. Together we turned on our flashlights and there on the floor was a young man crawling towards the corner of the room. At that time the father jumped out of bed and turned on the lights and asked what the hell was going on.

We arrested the burglar and were taking him out of the house when the other units found the house. The father stated he and his wife were in bed and the man crawling on the floor had awakened them, but they just laid still and watched him.

The other officers were a little upset with me, but when the Holy Spirit tells me something, I do it.

SAVED FROM HELL

I was working patrol division day watch on a warm Saturday afternoon. We had been looking for two guys for about three weeks. They had committed a robbery and murder. The main man I knew and I had arrested his wife before. He was mad at me for that. The suspect was a street heroin dealer and he himself was strung out on heroin.

Having run out of heroin, he and his wife along with a brother and two year old son went to get some heroin. He put a gun in his child's diaper when they went for some heroin. The suspect had a regular connection he bought from. After they got the heroin the suspect pulled out the gun and - while his wife, son and brother watched - robbed the victim of his heroin and money and shot him in the head. He was full of hate and hooked on heroin.

I had been checking all the places the suspect might visit. On this Saturday I found out that he would be getting into a certain car and going to rob and kill another heroin connection in just a few minutes. I was told that the suspect had a gun and said he would not go back to prison; he would shoot it out if he got caught.

I had only a few minutes before another murder would take place.

The first thing I did was to pray. I asked that no innocent person get hurt and that if this was the suspect's time to die that he not die until being born again. Then I got on the radio and rounded up some other officers. We had only a very few minutes before the suspect was going into action before leaving the state; this was according to reliable information I'd received.

I rounded up two patrol sergeants a four patrol officers. I was watching the vehicle the suspect was going to use and just as the first unit was getting close three men hurried into the vehicle and drove off. I followed them from a far distance in my black and white. We could not follow them without them knowing so we had to choose the safest spot to do a felony stop on the vehicle.

They headed into a residential neighborhood; we had to stop them before they entered it. We had only one spot to stop them. We all came up behind them rapidly and stopped them. There were seven of us and each one was a one man car; so, there were seven black and whites pulling into position behind them. They knew what was coming. We saw only two people in the car, figuring the suspect was hiding in the back seat. We stopped the vehicle and got the driver and passenger out. Suddenly, the suspect came rapidly out on the run in a crouched position. Both hands were in front of him; I could not see them. The suspect stopped and spun around with a gun in his hand and opened fire on us. He was pointing his gun at me; we were only about thirty feet apart. I was behind my car when he fired. I fired at the same time. The suspect took on all seven of us and it was apparent he wanted to die. I hit the suspect four times; the other officers also hit him. He was so loaded with heroin that he did not seem to feel anything. Finally he dropped to the ground after one of my shots caused the gun to fly out of his hand. We called the fire department; they came and took him to the hospital.

I stood in the street watching fire department drive away with him. Two medics were working on him. I watched and prayed he would not die at least until he was born again.

The report from the hospital was that the suspect would not live through the night. He was so mean that he told everyone who came near him that he was coming back to kill them: the firemen, doctors, nurses, anyone.

The next day in church the entire congregation prayed for the suspect. Monday morning he was still alive and was expected to die any time. Well, he lived to get to his preliminary hearing. He was in a wheel chair, green-colored skin. He was in bad condition.

While I was testifying about his attempt to kill me two girls in the audience would make remarks loud enough for the judge to hear. The judge stopped the hearing and ordered the two girls out; he had the bailiff remove them and find out who they were. The judge told the girls that if they came back into the courtroom they were going to jail. The Holy Spirit then told me to talk with the girls after court.

I got off the stand and went out to the hall where the girls were sitting on a bench. If looks could kill, I was dead. Well, I just forced my way in between them and sat down. I told them that the suspect had come out of the car shooting. I told them I did not want to shoot him but he shot first. It was obvious to us that he wanted us to kill him. I told them that I had been praying for him, along with my entire church. I said I was not mad at him and felt sorry for him. I asked them to have him talk with the jail chaplain.

I had said all that very quickly then stopped. They could not believe their ears. Their anger left and we talked for forty-five minutes. One of the girls was his sister and the other his friend. They were going to county jail and talk to him to check my story.

A few days later the sister came to the station looking for me. I just happened to be passing through the lobby when she came in. What luck; I think maybe not luck. She said they talked with her brother and he did want to die and he started the shooting. She said he was going to see the chaplain. She had told him I was not angry at him and was praying for him. About a week later she called me and said he was still alive and was talking with the chaplain a lot.

Well, he lived for trial in superior court. He had a jury trial. I was on the stand testifying. Every time I was asked a question he would nod in agreement. The jury noticed it; seemed almost comical. I would answer a question and he would nod, indicating I was telling the truth. The defense attorney did not notice it, nor did the district attorney. The jury would look at me and then at the suspect. This went on for about ten questions, then some legal point came up and the attorneys went to the side bar to privately discuss a legal point with the judge.

While they were talking, the suspect waved at me and said "Hi Harry." I quietly said Hi to him and called him by name. The jury looked a little puzzled. A few weeks ago we were shooting at each other on the street yet now it is like we are friends. I finished my testimony and left.

The suspect was one of the Satan's Soldiers; he killed one of his own and tried to kill me. His family was full of hatred and yet now he is saved. His name is in the lamb's book of life. It has changed his entire family. What Satan meant for evil the Lord has turned into good.

NO WAY TO SOLVE THIS ONE

I was working the afternoon shift in patrol division. It was just getting dark when we go11t a call of a possible body in the street. We were told that a person thought they saw a body in the street and drove home to call the police. They lived about three miles from where they thought they saw the body. It took us about one minute to get there.

When we pulled up we saw a woman's body in the street, by the curb. I checked her and she had been shot in the back. We called for the fire department. I noted the bullet had entered the center of her back and exited the front. I did what I could and I just sat in the street holding her in my arms. She died in my arms while hearing the fire department rushing to the scene. It was too late for her.

She had walked to the store and bought some ice cream and small donuts. She was headed back to her house where she and her nine year old daughter were staying. She and her daughter were going to eat ice cream and donuts and watch a Disney movie. The lady had been robbed then shot in the back. We had no witnesses and no evidence. We found one bullet cartridge on the ground in an alley about one hundred feet away from the victim. The bullet had passed through the victim; we could not find it.

The homicide detectives came to the scene and said that this case would never be solved. The Holy Spirit pointed out three young men in the crowd and told me they had killed the lady. It took me six months but I found the murder weapon and enough evidence for an arrest was collected. The suspects were convicted.

It was the Holy Spirit that solved the crime, not me.

TWENTY-EIGHT BANKS

There was this young man who had robbed 28 banks in the local area and everyone was looking for him. The different agencies had special details out turning over every rock and looking at all the know dope houses looking for this guy. The Holy Spirit told me to ask this one hooker about the guy, so I did. She told me he would be in our city and at a certain address in about one hour. She told me about the car he was driving and it matched the description of the suspect's car. She said she would get me the license number and have it in about half an hour. She knew a girl that knew the license number.

I contacted our detectives who were out looking everywhere for him and gave them the information. That was the proper thing to do as they were plain clothes and I was in uniform, driving a black and white. The detectives were not interested and did nothing with the information. I contacted one of my old partners who was working plain clothes at the time. He went to the address I was given.

As my partner drove into the area he saw the man we were looking for driving away. He had a passenger in the car. It was the guy that ran the dope house. We followed them and they pulled into a liquor store parking lot.

I rolled in quietly behind them and was standing at the rear of their car before they got out. I knew the name of the guy we were looking for and the fake name he was using. When the robber got out of the car I was there. He had a panicked look on his face so I played dumb. I told him the registration on the car was expired and his brake lights did not work. I asked him for his license and he said he left it at home. We talked and he gave me his fake name. I told him I was not going to give him a ticket but he needed to register the car and get the brake lights fixed. He got real relaxed. I told him good-by and he turned his back on me to walk away. I then told him it was not nice to rob banks and took him into custody. I kept my word; I did not give him a ticket.

I got on the radio and called the detectives who were looking for the suspect and a supervisor answered. I told them I knew where the suspect was now if they were interested. He got happy and said they were looking for him. I told them I could see him and what corner he was on. They replied not to let him out of my sight and they were on their way. I then told them he was wearing my handcuffs and he was not going anywhere without me.

The detectives rushed over and they swarmed the parking lot. I gave them the robber and went back to work.

GO GET HIM

I was working uniform patrol on the afternoon shift. The day before there had been a quadruple murder and one of the victims was only six months old. It was a stupid and violent thing, all about one person showing disrespect to another. Other family members got involved and tempers flared, leading to one man killing four people at one time. They had no weapons and the suspect just cold bloodedly shot and killed them all, including the six month old baby.

The suspect fled and was traced to a neighboring city. A huge task force was sent into that city along with that city's help. They looked everywhere but could not find the suspect. It was late in the afternoon and I was working that day. I was in the squad room for roll call when the captain came to me. He said the task force looking for the murder suspect was returning after a long day of looking. He told me to get out of uniform and into plain clothes and take my partner to help the neighboring city find the suspect. We changed clothes and got an undercover car. I was driving and we knew who we were looking for and what car he would probably be using. It was a large area to cover.

As we drove on the freeway the Holy Spirit told me where to get off the freeway and pointed out a small motel. I went into the office and showed the manager a photo of the suspect. He said he was in one of the rooms. He was positive, no doubt in his mind. He also described the car and it matched the car we thought he would be using.

I contacted the watch commander and advised him we found the location of the suspect, but we did not know if he was in the room now. We took a motel room where we could see his room and parking lot. The homicide detail sent out their team and came into our room through the back window. The homicide investigators took over the stakeout and we were there to assist them.

Awhile later one of the police units in the city we were in thought they may have the suspect at a bar about two miles from the motel and wanted one of our team to come and look at the person. One of the homicide team told me to come with him to the bar. In my spirit I just knew

I should stay there and I told them I should stay at the motel. Again, I was asked to go to the bar, almost an order now. Because I was under the authority of the homicide team I had to submit and go to the bar.

We went out the back window. My partner stayed at the motel. The person at the bar was not the suspect we were after so we started back to the motel. My partner came on the radio and stated a car matching the description of the car we were after had just pulled into the lot and a man that looked like the suspect's brother had gotten out of the car and gone into the room pointed out by the manager. About one minute later one of the homicide team came on the radio and said three men had come out of the room and were headed to the car. They said it looked like the suspect was with them. They were looking at the picture of the suspect, trying to make up their mind if it were him or not.

The Holy Spirit told me it was the one and I grabbed the radio and called my partner. I told him to go out and grab him. I repeated it over and over, but got no response. The men got into the car and left.

There had been a chase car supplied by the city police and one of their officers was in the motel room. He contacted the chase car. After the car exited they decided it was the suspect and radioed the chase car to intercept their car. The chase car could not find the car; the suspect got away.

I was angry and asked my partner why he did not go get the suspect in the parking lot. He said the homicide team would not allow it until they were sure. They did not want to give away the fact we had found the motel. The suspect never returned. It was not until about two years later before he was caught in another state.

Once the Holy Spirit told me what street to get off the freeway it was only about one minute before we were at the motel. I wondered why the suspect had been allowed to get away. All I know is that I am required to submit to the authority of those God has placed over me. In this case it was the homicide investigators.

EASY PICKINGS

I was on my bicycle on the way to work about 3 pm and the Holy Spirit directed me to go west on 3rd St from Cedar Ave. As I turned west onto 3rd St, a man came out of an apartment building and turned east, coming right at me. I recognized him as being wanted on a warrant for armed robbery.

I passed him, stopped my bicycle, got my gun and arrested him. We were only about one block from the police station so I walked him to the station. One of my command officers was standing on the front steps and asked me what I had this time. I told him and he said he would book him into jail so I could get into my uniform and get to the squad meeting.

Now some officers wondered why I would bother to arrest the man when I was off duty and had no backup.

What if I did not stop him and he committed another armed robbery and killed someone? Besides, the Holy Spirit was in control, no worries.

LIVES TO SAIL AGAIN

I was working uniform patrol day watch, assigned to the harbor area. It was around 10 am and the Holy Spirit directed me to go to Pier A, Berth one. So I did. I normally stayed away from there because they are busy loading and unloading ships.

I came around the end of the warehouse and saw a freighter from Japan just easing up to the dock. They were rigging the lines from the ship to the dock. On the stern I noted one seaman placing the lines over the cleats; one line did not go all the way on. The seaman was kicking it, trying to get it to fall over. The stern of the ship was now slowly moving away from the pier and tension was building on the line. Suddenly the line popped and the seaman flew straight up about thirty feet. His hard hat came off and flew into the water. He came crashing down on the iron cleats and steel deck.

He did not move; you could tell he was badly hurt. I called for the fire rescue. His shipmates came and picked him up. I used the public address system in my car to let the harbor department officers, who were there to see that the ship was properly moored, know what had happened. I told them to have the crew put the man down. They stopped the crew and laid the unconscious man on the deck. The fire department arrived and took him to a hospital.

A translator told us the crew was just going to put him in his bunk and take him back to Japan.

The doctor at the hospital said the man had broken bones and internal injuries. If he had not been brought to the hospital he would not have lived to make it to Japan.

REMEMBER ME?

I was going to work at about 6 am, riding my little Honda motorcycle when the Holy Spirit directed me to go down Long Beach Blvd. Headed that way I heard a burglar alarm start ringing on a bar and the door flew open. Two suspects came running out, dropping money. I followed them into the alley and one suspect got in the driver's seat of a car and drove off, leaving the other behind. I saw the driver and got the license number. I followed the other suspect for five blocks before he got too tired to go on. I was on my motorcycle, so I was fine.

I walked him back to the bar and a patrol unit was pulling up in response to the alarm. I turned the suspect over to them and went to the station to meet my partner.

We were on special assignment that day, assisting the probation department. (We did early morning searches for people thought to be in violation of probation. Each morning we did two searches and then went back to our regular jobs.) I walked in and my partner gave me the paperwork of that day's two searches. I looked at the first and noted it was the owner of the car that had fled from the bar a few minutes ago. We had a photo of the owner of the vehicle and it was the suspect I saw run from the bar and drive away. I told my partner about the bar burglary and we went on the search.

When we pulled up to the house, there was the car. We knocked on the door and the suspect opened it. I said "Remember Me?"

THE COMPTON FIVE

I was working afternoon patrol watch and was in the station at the records division desk looking up the record of a person when a homicide detective from the city of Compton walked up. He was investigating a murder and knew who one suspect was but there were five others and he had no idea who they were. He asked me if I could help.

I knew the one suspect and instantly the Holy Spirit told me who the others were. I gave their names to him. He got their files from our records division.

A few weeks later I ran into the detective again and he told me that those were the five he was looking for. He got them identified and were now in custody.

THE BOY'S MARKET
ROBBERS

I was working uniform patrol afternoon watch and in the squad room waiting for roll call. One of my command officers came over and asked me about all the robberies occurring in The Boys Market parking lot at 36rh St and Atlantic Ave. People were being robbed in and around the parking lot in the early evenings on a regular basis.

I told him it was too far from my beat to work it and the units in the area are not going about it properly. I also told him that they were going to strike today; the Holy Spirit had just told me. He told me to get into plain clothes with my partner and get a plain car to cover the area.

We got set up at 36th St and Atlantic Ave., each of us in our own spot as directed by the Holy Spirit. About ten minutes later here they came. To make a long story short, we arrested the suspects. They admitted that the rash of robberies was an "initiation" into a gang and a gang member must witness the robbery. The robberies stopped.

7TH ST MURDER SUSPECT

I was working a plain clothes unit out of afternoon patrol division. One of our homicide detectives came to me for help. There had been a murder in a house on 7th St and the investigation had stalled. He gave me all the facts and said not to worry about anything; but, they were at a standstill and anything that I did would not hurt the investigation.

That night we took bicycles with us. About 10 pm the Holy Spirit told me to go to the murder scene. We rode the bikes to the scene.

Looking up at the penthouse where the murder occurred was a man who exactly matched the suspect description, right down to the same clothes and odd little hat.

He stood there looking up for a good minute or so and then walked away. We followed him for about twenty minutes. We had enough to at least detain him but I wanted more. Finally, he committed misdemeanor and we contacted him. We took him to the station and the homicide team came in and took custody of him. He was charged and tried for the murder.

THE BROADWAY BURGLAR

We were working a plain clothes unit out of patrol division. Again, the Holy Spirit directed me to go to Broadway and Orange Ave. Once there, the Holy Spirit pointed out a man walking east on Broadway on the north side of the street. We followed him a few blocks when he stopped and looked around; then he went north between a house and a fence, leaving the street.

We closed in and he came running out. My partner went after him; I looked at the window screen. It had been freshly cut and a person inside had spooked him. We chased the suspect for three blocks and caught up. He fought; we took him to the ground and handcuffed him. Just then, a man walked up and looked at the suspect and said that was the person who tried to get into his apartment last night. He had cut the screen and was coming in the window. He ran the guy off. He filed a police report on the crime.

THE QUINCY BURGLAR

We were in plain clothes. About 11 pm one night I had driven to the Belmont Shore area of Long Beach and the Holy Spirit pointed out a man and said to watch him. We followed him on foot for about thirty minutes when he went into the residential area. He went up Quincy Ave and disappeared behind some bushes.

We stopped and listened. You could hear a wire screen being cut so we moved in. He saw us and dropped down behind the bushes. I heard a heavy metal object hit the ground. I knew it was a gun. We arrested him and got the gun. He had just cut through a wire window screen.

A very old lady lived there alone. I hate to think what might have happened if we had not been there.

ARTESIA BAR ROBBERY AND RAPE

We were in plain clothes, working out of patrol division. I was made aware of an armed robbery of a bar on Artesia St. The robbery include a kidnapping of the bar maid; they left her naked in Compton.

The Holy Spirit told me to go to the area they had left the bar maid. I drove down one street and the Spirit pointed out a parked car. I ran the license number and there was a felony "stop for armed robbery" from the city of Buena Park. Their suspect description was the same as our two suspects. We notified Buena Park and two detectives came out.

The suspects had borrowed the car from the owner. We were able to provide enough information for our detectives to follow up and handle the case.